COOL CLAY

✔ **W9-ANR-919**

MUD PUDDLE BOOKS, INC.
New York, New York

Published by
Mud Puddle Books, Inc.
54 W. 21st Street
Suite 601
New York, NY 10010 USA

info@mudpuddlebooks.com

Hinkler Books Pty Ltd
17 – 23 Redwood Drive
Dingley Victoria 3172 Australia
www.hinklerbooks.com

© Hinkler Books Pty Ltd 2004

Written by: Heather Hammonds
Design: Monitor Graphics

ISBN: 1 59412 040 4

Printed and bound in China.

CONTENTS

INTRODUCTION

Clay modeling is a popular and exciting art form. You can enjoy hours of fun making a huge variety of objects, from the simplest shapes through to complex sculptures of people and scenes.

You are limited only by your imagination!

Modeling has a history that goes back thousands of years, in all parts of the world. Ancient people created basic clay pots for cooking and storing goods. They also created small clay models of human forms, as well as the animals they saw around them. Beads and other ornaments were also made from clay. Many of these items have been found in ancient graves and they help us learn about people of the past.

They probably had just as much fun working with clay as we do today.

Today, modeling is more popular than ever. New modeling materials that do not dry out quickly have opened up a whole new creative world for modelers. Turn the pages of this book and step into the exciting world of modeling. Invent some of your own creatures and characters. Build pots, people – whatever you like. Once you start clay modeling, we're sure you'll love it!

TYPES OF CLAY

You can use several different types of clay when modeling. Some are easier to use than others. Some need to be 'fired' in a special kiln (like a very hot oven), or baked in an oven to harden them. Others stay soft and never harden, so you can use them again and again.

Modeling Clay

Modeling clay has a base of waxes or oils, or petroleum jelly. It is completely non-toxic and safe to use. It has been used for about 100 years and is probably the most popular. It will not harden, so you can use it many times to make lots of different models.

Earth Clay

Earth clay is also known as natural clay. It is dug from the earth and is the oldest modeling material. Earth clay models must be dried out and then fired in a hot kiln, to harden them.

Doughs

Clay doughs and salt doughs are softer than modeling clay, and are used in similar ways. They can be bought or you can make them at home. Some can be heated in the oven to make them last a long time. Others can be used over and over again.

Polymer Clays

Polymer clays can be bought in kits at craft stores and must be heated in an oven to harden them. They do not shrink when baked, which some doughs do. They also come in a great range of bright colors.

TYPES OF CLAY

To get the best out of your clays, you need to know how to look after them!

Modeling Clay

Modeling clay never dries out. However, dirt just loves to stick to it, so always work on a clean surface when you're modeling. If unwanted bits of clay stick to modeling tools, simply wash them off in hot soapy water. Store modeling clay in plastic wrap or plastic bags when not in use.

Earth Clay

Earth clay dries out very easily. Wrap it in a wet cloth and store it in an airtight container when not in use. Earth clay can easily be cleaned up with water. Dry earth clay dust should always be wiped up with a damp cloth, rather than brushed away. Ask an adult to help you, as breathing in clay dust may be harmful.

Doughs

Clay doughs you buy can be re-used many times. They will eventually dry out, but will last a long time if stored in their containers when not in use. Home-made doughs will last from two days to around a week, depending on the recipe. Store them in the fridge. They are easily cleaned up with soap and water.

Polymer Clays

Polymer clays will stay soft until you bake them in an oven. Always ask an adult to help you bake your models, and follow the instructions on your brand of polymer clay. Store polymer clays in airtight containers when not in use.

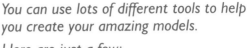

MODELING TOOLS

You can use lots of different tools to help you create your amazing models.

Here are just a few:

Knives and Forks
Table knives and forks are great for cutting, shaping and making patterns on clay. Always use rounded knives, such as butter knives. They are the safest.

Rolling Pin
A small rolling pin is very handy for flattening out pieces of clay, especially when you are creating two-dimensional scenes or flat ribbons.

Jars of Different Sizes
You can use glass or plastic jars as a template, to trace around when you need a perfect circle for your projects.

Toothpicks
Toothpicks can be used to create small holes in clay, or create marks and patterns on clay.

Ice Cream Sticks
Wooden ice cream sticks are great for creating interesting patterns on clay. You can also use their flat edges for smoothing out clay.

MODELING TOOLS

Pencils
You can use sharp pointed pencils to create marks and patterns on clay. The rounded end of a pencil also creates interesting patterns.

Garlic Press
Strange as it sounds, a garlic press is one of the most useful tools when clay modeling! Use it to create "hair", "grass" and anything that requires lots of small strands of clay.

Skewers
As with a sharp pointed pencil or a toothpick, you can create patterns on clay with the end of a skewer. Skewers are also very useful at times when you need to make holes in clay, such as when you are making clay beads.

Stencils
You can use stencils to create shapes or letters on clay. Then you can cut out the shapes. Letter stencils are particularly useful, when you want to write a name in clay.

Modeling Tool Kits
If you want to take modeling further, you can buy a set of professional modeling tools from an art or craft store. These contain small knives, spatulas etc. that are specially made for modeling.

Now that you know all about clays, how to care for them and the tools you'll need, it's time to get started. When you first begin modeling you need to practice creating a few simple shapes. These shapes will form the basis of many of your models.

Ball

The ball is the most important shape you will ever make when modeling. It is the basis of many other shapes and it should also be used when first working with a piece of new clay. This is especially important when using modeling clay because the waxes and oils in the clay are softened by the heat of your hands as you shape the clay, and this makes it easier to work with.

Squash a piece of clay together with your fingers and then gently roll it into a ball between the palms of your hands, until it is smooth and there are no lines showing.

You must apply even pressure with both hands to get a perfect ball shape – practice hard and you'll soon be able to do it.

Cone

Cone shapes are used to make hats, animal heads and a host of other model parts.

Create a cone from a ball by carefully pinching the end of a ball into a point. Then roll it gently a couple of times between your palms to keep the base round. Finally, squash the rounded end of your ball onto a flat surface. You have a cone!

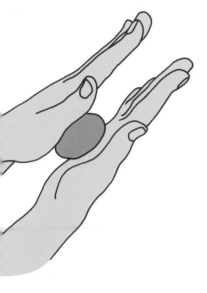

Oval

The oval shape is a variation of the ball and it is very useful for creating some animal and people bodies. It can also be used to create the heads of some animals – as well as eggs, which are featured later in this book.

Take a ball of clay and roll it back and forth between your hands, pressing a little more firmly than you would with a regular ball shape. Do this until the ball becomes longer and you see both ends becoming slightly narrower. This takes practice, as you need to get the pressure of your hands just right, to form a good oval shape. You'll soon get it right!

Sausage

Thick sausage shapes can be used to create animal and people bodies, and are almost as important as the ball shape. You can make them in many different sizes, to suit whatever model you wish to make.

Take a ball of clay and roll it back and forth between your hands until it becomes longer and forms a thick sausage. Then place it on a flat surface and continue to roll it until it is the exact thickness and length that you want it to be. If you wish to, you can tidy up the ends of a sausage by cutting them off with a knife. Or you can simply pinch them off neatly.

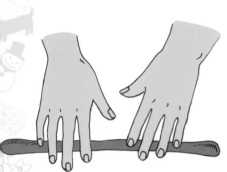

Rope

Rope shapes are very useful indeed. They are used to make snakes, coil pots and many other things. It takes a little practice to get clay ropes which are of an even thickness, but you can have fun learning how to do it.

Lay a ball on a flat surface and use both palms of your hands to roll and stretch the ball out into a rope, until it is of the required thickness and length. Be sure to apply equal pressure with both palms, so your rope is of an even thickness at both ends.

Ribbon

Ribbon shapes are a very important variation of the rope shape. They can be used when creating flat two-dimensional pictures, as well as making bridges, bows, handles etc. Simply make a rope shape and then use a small rolling pin to flatten it out, into a ribbon! Take care to press evenly with the rolling pin, so that the edges of the ribbon stay straight. When first making ribbons, don't make the rope shape too thin. Very thin ropes tend to break, or stick to the work surface when flattened out.

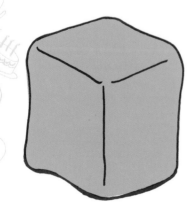

Cube

Cube shapes are used for making objects such as cakes, houses and cars. The cube can easily be made from a ball. Use a flat object such as the flat side of a table knife (be sure to use a knife with a rounded end that is not sharp!) to push down on the top of the ball and flatten it. Turn the ball over and flatten again, until all six sides are flat and even. Now you have a cube!

Rectangular Block

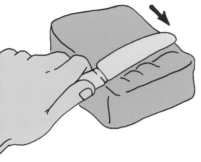

Rectangular blocks are perfect when you need a shape just that little bit longer than a cube! You can use them to make parts of buildings, cars and other machines. Or use them in the same way as you would a sausage, to make animal and people bodies.

Rectangular blocks are made by first rolling a sausage shape. Then use a flat object such as the flat side of a table knife to push down the top of the sausage and flatten it.

Turn the sausage over and flatten again, until all the long sides of the block are flat and even. Cut the ends of the rectangular block neatly with the knife, to finish it off.

Square and Round Slabs

Square and round slab shapes have many uses. For instance, they can be used to make the walls of pots, or as a base to stand your models on. Simply use a rolling pin to roll a ball of clay out evenly on a flat surface. To make a square slab, cut out a square with a knife. To make a round slab, stand a round jar on top of the clay and cut around it.

Small Circle

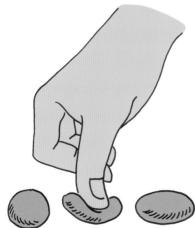

Small circles are often used on smaller models, instead of the round slab. They are great for making objects such as the wheels of little cars or the base of hats. Take a small ball of clay and place it on a flat surface. Then press it down with your thumb, until it is the desired thickness.

FIRST PROJECTS

Once you've learnt to make simple shapes, try some of these first projects. They're easy to make and look fantastic. They will also help you practice modeling, so you can go on to make some of the more difficult projects in this book.

PINCH POT

Pinch pots have been made for thousands of years and it is believed they may have been the first types of pots ever made!

YOU WILL NEED:

- Modeling clay in the color of your choice
- Knife

1. First, roll some clay into a large ball, working the ball until it is nice and smooth.
2. Place the ball on a table or other flat work surface and then push your thumb into the center of the ball.
3. Use your thumbs and fingers to pinch up the sides of the ball, turning the ball as you work so that the sides of the pot are all even. Take care not to make the walls of the pot too thin.
4. When you have pinched out the pot to the height you want it, press gently on the bottom to make the base of the pot flat.
5. Use the knife to trim the top of the pot, so it is flat and even. You're done!

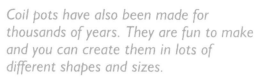

COIL POT

Coil pots have also been made for thousands of years. They are fun to make and you can create them in lots of different shapes and sizes.

YOU WILL NEED:

- Modeling clay in the color of your choice
- Rolling pin, small jar and knife

1. First make a round slab by rolling a piece of clay out and cutting around a small jar, as shown on Page 11.

2. Now make some long thin ropes by rolling out some balls, as shown on Page 10. Make all the ropes around the same thickness.

3. Place one end of the first rope on the round slab and wind it slowly around. You will see that the rope is forming the walls of your pot.

4. Add another rope, squashing the two ends of the ropes together so that the wall of the pot doesn't have any holes in it. Keep adding clay ropes until the pot is as big as you want it to be.

5. Gently squash the end of the top rope against the wall, so that the top of the pot is even. Smooth the coils together on the inside of the pot a little with your fingers, so that the coils do not come apart. Your pot is finished!

TIP!

We've used modeling clay to make many of the projects in this book, but they can be made using any of the clays mentioned on Page 4.

HOODED COBRA

Hooded Cobras are the dangerous snakes that snake charmers love to keep. You can create your own fearsome cobra. Here's how:

YOU WILL NEED:

- Dark colored modeling clay in the color of your choice
- Small amount of white modeling clay
- Toothpick
- Knife

1. First, roll some clay into a ball and then begin to roll out a rope shape, as shown on Page 10.

2. As you roll out the rope, press harder with your left hand so that one end of the rope becomes thinner. This is the snake's tail. Do not press as hard with your right hand, so that the other end of the rope is thicker. Leave the very end of the thicker part of the rope much thicker. This is the snake's head.

3. Now roll two very small balls of clay and place them on the snake's head – these are its eyes. Then use the toothpick to make a line for its mouth. Finally, roll out a very thin piece of white clay rope and break off two little pieces. Attach them to its mouth – these are its fangs!

4. To make the cobra's hood simply pinch out each side of the snake's neck, slightly behind the head. Simple! Try making lots of snakes in different sizes.

SMILING SNOWMAN

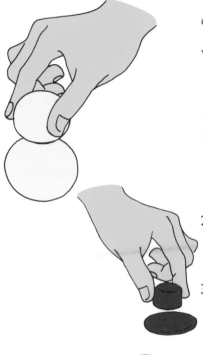

This fun snowman makes a cool decoration at Christmas time.

YOU WILL NEED:
- White modeling clay
- Black modeling clay
- Knife
- 2 toothpicks

1. First, roll two balls of white clay until they are smooth. One ball of clay should be bigger than the other.

2. Place the smallest ball on top of the largest and press them together, so they stick together. You now have the basis of your snowman.

3. Cut a small piece off the end of the stick of black clay. This is the top of the snowman's hat. Then roll a piece of black clay into a ball and form a small circle, as shown on Page 11. This is the brim of the snowman's hat. Stick the two pieces together and place the hat on the snowman's head.

4. Roll some tiny balls of black clay for the snowman's eyes and buttons. Roll a tiny rope and make a smiley mouth.

5. Finally, give your snowman two toothpick arms and he is complete.

TIP!

Keep your snowman away from sources of heat, such as a radiator.

Just like real snow, modeling clay melts when it is heated!

CUTE TORTOISE

This little tortoise makes a cute pet. Make one for yourself and then some for your friends.

YOU WILL NEED:
- Dark colored modeling clay
- Green modeling clay
- Toothpick or pencil

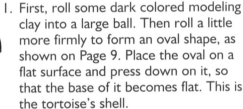

1. First, roll some dark colored modeling clay into a large ball. Then roll a little more firmly to form an oval shape, as shown on Page 9. Place the oval on a flat surface and press down on it, so that the base of it becomes flat. This is the tortoise's shell.

2. Take a smaller amount of green clay and roll it into a smaller ball. Flatten the base of the ball as you would for a cone shape. This will become the tortoise's head.

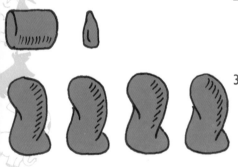

3. Now make a thick green rope, as shown on Page 10. Cut a small piece – this will be the tortoise's neck. Cut a very small piece and squeeze the end of it to make a little triangle shape – this will be his tail. Cut 4 longer pieces of equal length and bend them a little – these will be his legs.

4. Join all the pieces of the tortoise together, as shown.

5. Use the toothpick or pencil to carefully decorate the back of the tortoise, and draw in his eyes and mouth. And there you have it – a new pet!

LITTLE LADYBIRD

Here's another exciting first project that you'll love to make.

YOU WILL NEED:
- Bright red modeling clay
- Black modeling clay
- Knife

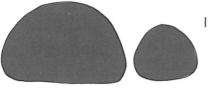

1. First, roll and knead the stick of red clay into a ball. Then roll the ball into an oval shape, as shown on Page 9. Place the oval on a flat surface and press down on it, so that the base of it becomes flat. This is the ladybird's body.

2. Take some black clay and roll it into a ball. Flatten the base of the ball, as you would when forming a cone shape. Then stick it to one end of the red oval. This is the ladybird's head.

3. Roll some more black clay out into a thin rope shape, as shown on Page 10. Use the knife to cut the rope into six even parts. Then attach three to each side of the ladybird and bend them over a little. These are its legs and feet.

4. Roll another very thin black rope and make two antennae for the ladybird. Attach them to its head. Roll four little balls – two for its eyes and two for the top of its antennae.

5. Finally, make lots of very small black circles as shown on Page 11, and attach them to the ladybird's back. Your ladybird is complete!

TIP

Try making the tortoise and ladybird in other, bright colors.

FUN FOOD

When you make these fun food projects they'll look good enough to eat... but don't try it. After all, they're only made of modeling clay!

CRAZY COOKIES

Serve these tiny cookies up to your dolls, or stick them on your desk as a fun decoration.

YOU WILL NEED:

- Black or brown modeling clay
- White modeling clay
- Yellow modeling clay
- Rolling pin, knife, small jar and plastic bottle cap

1. First, roll the yellow clay into a smooth ball. Then use the rolling pin, knife and jar to make a round slab, as shown on Page 11. This is the plate.

2. Now take some black or brown clay and roll it into a smooth ball. Use the rolling pin to roll out the clay until it is flat.

3. Use the round plastic bottle cap as a cookie cutter. Cut ten cookies out of the clay.

4. Take some white clay and roll it into a smooth ball. Roll the clay out very thinly. Then cut five circles out of it. You now have cream for the cookies.

5. Stick the cookies together with the cream in the center as shown. Yum!

TIP!

Try making other types of cookies, such as chocolate chip.

CAKE AND CANDLES

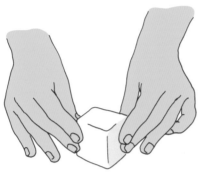

Why not make a modeling clay birthday cake as a special gift the next time one of your friends has a birthday?

YOU WILL NEED:

- White modeling clay
- Blue or pink modeling clay
- Red modeling clay
- Knife
- 4 toothpicks
- Small piece of aluminum foil

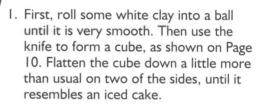

1. First, roll some white clay into a ball until it is very smooth. Then use the knife to form a cube, as shown on Page 10. Flatten the cube down a little more than usual on two of the sides, until it resembles an iced cake.

2. Fold the piece of aluminum foil into a neat square, so it looks like a cake tray. Then stand the cube on it.

3. Roll a very thin rope, using either pink or blue clay. Pink for girls, blue for boys. Carefully place the rope around the base of the cake.

4. Place a toothpick on each of the four corners of the cake. Break the toothpicks and make them shorter if they seem too long.

5. Finally, roll four tiny balls of red clay and place them on top of each toothpick. Your cake is finished and the candles are lit!

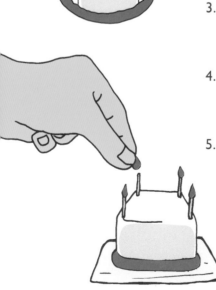

HOT DOGS

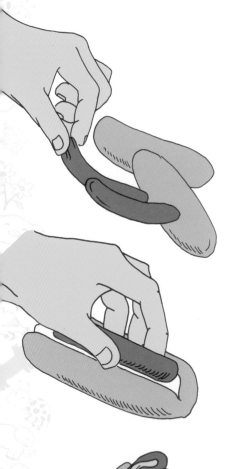

These hot dogs will make your mouth water. Don't forget the mustard!

YOU WILL NEED:

- White or light brown modeling clay
- Red modeling clay
- Yellow modeling clay
- Knife

1. First, use the white or light brown clay to make two thick sausage shapes, as shown on Page 9. Pinch and mold the ends until they are round, so that they look like long hot dog rolls.

2. Now roll two balls of red clay, until they are smooth. Make each ball into a rope shape, as shown on Page 10. Make the rope shapes so they are the same length as the roll shapes. Pinch and mold the ends of the rope shapes until they are rounded, and the rope shapes look like hot dogs.

3. Use the knife to carefully cut a line down the center of each of the roll shapes. Be careful not to cut all the way through them.

4. Gently push the two halves of the roll shapes apart with your fingers and slip the red hot dogs inside them, as shown.

5. Make two very thin ropes of yellow clay. Then carefully lay them in a zigzag pattern across the top of each of the hot dogs. Your hot dogs are ready!

FRENCH FRIES

Serve these funny French fries with hot dog or burger models. They're quick to make and look terrific.

YOU WILL NEED:

- Yellow modeling clay
- White modeling clay
- Rolling pin, knife and small jar

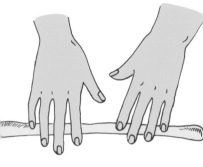

1. First, roll the white clay into a smooth ball. Then use the rolling pin, knife and jar to make a round slab, as shown on Page 11. This is the plate.

2. Now take the yellow clay and make some fries. Roll lots of small thin ropes, as shown on Page 10.

3. Use your knife to cut each rope into lengths that will fit neatly on the plate. Cut them on an angle, just like real fries.

4. Carefully flatten the sides of the ropes, so that each piece of rope has four flat sides.

5. Arrange the fries on the plate. They almost look good enough to eat!

TIP!

Mini foods like the ones featured on these pages also look great when made from bright polymer clays.

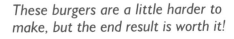

MINI BURGERS

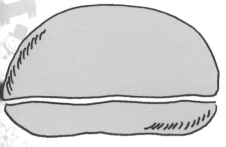

These burgers are a little harder to make, but the end result is worth it!

YOU WILL NEED:

- White or light brown modeling clay
- Dark brown or black modeling clay
- Red, green and orange modeling clay
- Blue modeling clay
- Rolling pin, knife, smaller jar and larger jar
- Garlic press

1. First, let's make the burger bun! Roll two balls of white or light brown clay, of around the same size. Place one ball on a flat surface and press down on it, so that the base of it becomes flat. Then use the rolling pin, knife and smaller jar to make a round slab with the other ball, as shown on page 11.

2. Now let's put some meat in the burger. Use dark brown clay for a medium burger or black clay for a well done burger. Roll a ball of clay and then make another round slab with the smaller jar, the same size as the base of the burger bun you made in Step 1.

3. To make the lettuce for the burger, place a ball of green clay in the garlic press and make lots of thin green strands. Then use the rolling pin to gently flatten the strands.

4. Make some grated carrot for the burger by placing a ball of orange clay into the garlic press and making lots of thin orange strands. Again, use the rolling pin to gently flatten the strands.

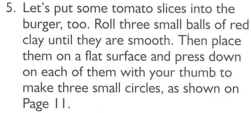

5. Let's put some tomato slices into the burger, too. Roll three small balls of red clay until they are smooth. Then place them on a flat surface and press down on each of them with your thumb to make three small circles, as shown on Page 11.

6. Use some white clay to make three or four very small thin ribbons, as shown on Page 10. Join the ends of the ribbons together and you have some onion rings.

7. Now assemble the burger. Place the round meat slab on top of the flat round bun slab. Sprinkle some lettuce on top of the meat. Then do the same with the carrot. Carefully place the tomato slices and onion rings on top of the meat, lettuce and carrot. Finally, put the top of the bun on the burger.

8. To finish your model off, roll a ball of blue clay. Then use the rolling pin, knife and larger jar to make a larger round slab. This is the plate.

9. Stand your finished burger on the plate. Then admire your cool creation!

TIP!

If you are using more than one color clay in a garlic press during a project, wash the press between each color.

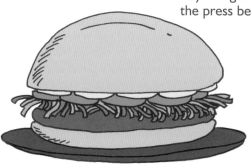

BOWL OF FRUIT

Let's create a bowl of fruit with lots of bright, cheerful colors and a pretty pinch pot!

YOU WILL NEED:

- White modeling clay
- Orange modeling clay
- Red modeling clay
- Light green modeling clay
- Dark green modeling clay
- Black or brown modeling clay
- Yellow modeling clay
- Knife and toothpick

1. Roll a large ball of white clay until it is nice and smooth. Then pinch and mold it into a pinch pot, as shown on Page 12. Keep the sides of the pinch pot low and the base of the pinch pot wide so that it is formed into a little bowl. Pressing out more with your thumbs as you work the clay ball helps to do this.

2. Now let's make some fruit to fill the bowl. Roll two small balls of orange clay, until they are smooth and round. Use the toothpick to make a little round mark in the top of each ball. You now have two oranges. Simple!

3. Next, roll two smaller balls of red clay, until they are smooth and round. Then take a small piece of light green clay and roll two ropes, as shown on Page 10. Make the ropes very small and thin. Cut two pieces of rope and stick them to the tops of the red balls. Then join the top of the ropes together. You now have two cherries.

4. Now roll two dark green balls until they are smooth and round. Take a very small piece of black or brown clay and roll into a tiny, thin rope. Cut two short pieces from the rope and stick one to the top of each green ball. You now have two apples, complete with stalks on the top.

5. What would a fruit bowl be without bananas? Take some yellow clay and make a rope, as shown on Page 10. Make the rope as thick as you want the bananas to be. Now cut two banana-sized lengths from the rope. Use the knife to smooth the sides of the ropes so that they are flatter, like a banana skin. Then carefully pinch and mold the end of each rope to form the top and bottom of the bananas.

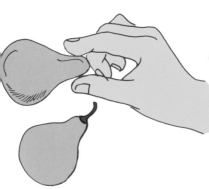

6. Create two pears using light green clay. Roll two small balls until they are smooth and then create a cone shape, as shown on Page 8. However, do not squash the rounded end of the ball onto a flat surface, as you do when making a regular cone. Then take a very small piece of black or brown clay and roll into a tiny, thin rope. Cut two short pieces from the rope and stick one to the top of each green cone, for stalks.

7. Arrange all your fruit neatly in the bowl. Looks great, doesn't it?

TIP!

When you have completed your bowl of fruit, stand it on the kitchen windowsill, so the whole family can admire your handiwork!

IN THE GARDEN

You can make all sorts of wonderful models based on plants and animals in the garden. Here are three to get you started.

BIRD AND NEST

YOU WILL NEED:

- Black or brown modeling clay
- White modeling clay
- Yellow modeling clay
- Orange modeling clay
- Rolling pin, knife and small jar
- Garlic press and toothpick

1. First, let's make the bird – a bright yellow and orange canary. Roll two balls of yellow clay until they are smooth. One ball should be bigger than the other.

2. Roll the largest ball into an oval, as shown on Page 9. Then pinch one end of the oval, spreading it out to form a tail. Place the smaller ball on the front of the oval, to make a head.

3. Roll a small amount of orange clay into a ball and form a cone shape, as shown on Page 8. This is the bird's beak. Stick it on to the bird's head.

4. Use some more orange clay to make two small circles as shown on Page 11. Then pinch and mold them into wing shapes, to form two flat wings. Attach the wings to the body, then use the toothpick to create two eyes. Your bird is finished!

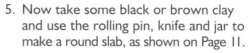

5. Now take some black or brown clay and use the rolling pin, knife and jar to make a round slab, as shown on Page 11.

6. Use some more black clay to make a long thin rope, as shown on Page 10. Place one end of the rope on the round slab and coil it around, two to three times, until you have a shallow coil pot. This is the basis of the bird's nest.

7. Place some black or brown clay into the garlic press and make lots of thin black strands. These are the sticks in the nest. Stick them all around the outside and inside of the nest.

8. Finally, use the white clay to make four small ovals. Roll the ovals so that they become egg-shaped and place them into the nest. Your canary now has some eggs in her nest!

TIP!

Try making colorful parrots and other birds, using different colored modeling clay.

POT OF FLOWERS

This colorful model is easy to make and it will brighten up any room.

YOU WILL NEED:

- Purple modeling clay
- Green modeling clay
- More modeling clay in bright colors – we suggest red, orange and yellow
- Rolling pin, knife and jar
- Garlic press

1. First, use the purple clay to make a small coil pot, as shown on Page 13. Wind the clay coils around the pot three or four times, pushing them slightly outwards so the top of the pot is a little wider than the bottom.

2. Now place a ball of green clay into the garlic press and squeeze the press together, so that you make lots of thin clay strands.

3. Carefully separate each of the green strands and lay them out, so that you have at least fifteen of them. Try to have them all around the same length. They will form the flower stalks.

4. Now use your choice of brightly colored clays to make fifteen (or more) tiny clay balls. These will form the flower blooms.

5. Take each of the colored balls and press them onto the tops of the green stalks, so they become flat, like the small circles we showed you how to make on Page 11. Don't make the blooms too big, or the stalks will bend and break when you arrange them in the pot.

6. Arrange all the flowers in the pot. Start by putting a row around the edge of the pot. Press the bottom of each of the stalks to the base of the pot, to hold the flowers in place.

7. Now add more flowers, working around the pot in circles, until you have filled it up. Remember to gently attach the bottom of each stalk to the base of the pot. Your project is now complete!

TIP!

When working with very small pieces of modeling clay like these flowers, they sometimes become too soft to work with – especially on hot days. If this happens, simply put the clay in the fridge for a short time.

COLORFUL BLOOMS

You can make flat, two-dimensional scenes with clay, too. These beautiful flowers are just one example.

YOU WILL NEED:

- Small piece of square cardboard or wooden board (alternatively, a thin square slab of modeling clay)
- Green modeling clay
- Red and yellow modeling clay
- Pink and white modeling clay
- Rolling pin, knife and garlic press

1. First, roll two larger balls and two smaller balls of green modeling clay, until they are smooth. Then make two longer green ribbons and two shorter, thinner green ribbons, as shown on page 10.

2. Carefully place the ribbons onto the piece of cardboard – two in the center and two in the outside corners, as shown. These are the flower stalks.

3. Use the garlic press to make lots and lots of strands of green grass – some longer and some shorter.

4. Separate the strands of grass and use the rolling pin to gently roll them flat. Then arrange them onto your scene, as shown. Put the taller grass in the center, around the taller stalks. Put the shorter grass towards the edges, around the shorter stalks.

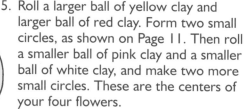

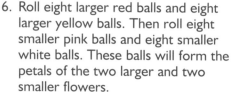

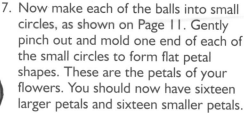

5. Roll a larger ball of yellow clay and larger ball of red clay. Form two small circles, as shown on Page 11. Then roll a smaller ball of pink clay and a smaller ball of white clay, and make two more small circles. These are the centers of your four flowers.

6. Roll eight larger red balls and eight larger yellow balls. Then roll eight smaller pink balls and eight smaller white balls. These balls will form the petals of the two larger and two smaller flowers.

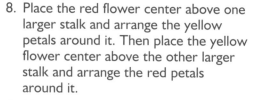

7. Now make each of the balls into small circles, as shown on Page 11. Gently pinch out and mold one end of each of the small circles to form flat petal shapes. These are the petals of your flowers. You should now have sixteen larger petals and sixteen smaller petals.

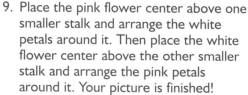

8. Place the red flower center above one larger stalk and arrange the yellow petals around it. Then place the yellow flower center above the other larger stalk and arrange the red petals around it.

9. Place the pink flower center above one smaller stalk and arrange the white petals around it. Then place the white flower center above the other smaller stalk and arrange the pink petals around it. Your picture is finished!

TIP!

You can make lots of flat, two-dimensional scenes. Try making houses, people and cars, too.

HAPPY HALLOWEEN

Halloween is the spookiest time of the year – and you can make some creepy models to scare your friends and family.

GHOSTLY GHOULS

YOU WILL NEED:

- White modeling clay
- Toothpick

1. Roll a large ball of white clay until it is nice and smooth. Then form a large oval, as shown on Page 9. Place the oval on a flat surface and push down on it, to flatten the bottom. This is the body of your ghostly ghoul.

2. Now pinch and mold the top quarter of the body until you form a head shape, as shown.

3. Carefully pinch and mold out two ghostly arms from each side of the body. Be sure to pinch an equal amount of clay from each side of the model, as you form the arms.

4. Pinch and pull a small amount of clay out from the head, to form a nose. Then use the toothpick to create the eyes and mouth. Your ghoul is finished. Scary, isn't it?

TIP!

Ask an adult to take a photo of your modeling projects. Then if they get damaged or you make something else with the clay, you will have a record of what they looked like.

JACK O LANTERN

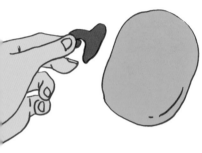

Halloween just wouldn't be the same without a Jack O Lantern. This model is easy to make. Why not make some for your friends?

YOU WILL NEED:

- Orange modeling clay
- Green modeling clay
- Red modeling clay
- Rolling pin and knife
- Pencil

1. First, roll a ball of orange clay until it is smooth. Press it down slightly on a flat surface, to flatten the top and bottom of the ball a little.

2. Use the green clay to create a small cone shape, as shown on Page 8. Pinch and twist the top of the cone into a thick stalk. Then place the stalk on top of the pumpkin.

3. Using the pencil, carefully create thin lines around the top sides of the pumpkin to divide it into segments, just like a real pumpkin.

4. Roll out the red clay with the rolling pin, to form a thin, flat slab. Then cut out three very small triangles with the knife. These are the eyes and nose of the Jack O Lantern. Cut out a red mouth, too.

5. Stick the eyes and mouth to the pumpkin and your spooky Jack O Lantern is ready for Halloween!

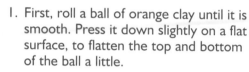

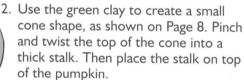

With her long nose, pointy chin and old straw broom, this Halloween witch is truly creepy. This project takes a little longer to make, but it is worth the effort.

YOU WILL NEED:

- Purple modeling clay
- Black modeling clay
- Green modeling clay
- Yellow modeling clay
- Garlic press and knife

1. First, roll and knead a large ball of purple clay, until it is smooth. Then roll the ball into a cone shape, as shown on Page 8. This will become the witch's cape.

2. Pinch and mold the top of the cone until you have formed shoulders and a neck. Don't make the neck too thin, or the witch's head will be unable to sit on it.

3. Slightly flatten each side of the cone shape with the knife, to form the witch's front and back. Making the cape takes a little practice, so play around with it until you are happy that you have a good shape.

4. Next, roll some green clay to form a smooth ball. Then form an oval shape, as shown on Page 9. This will be the witch's head.

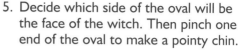
5. Decide which side of the oval will be the face of the witch. Then pinch one end of the oval to make a pointy chin.

6. Halfway up the face, pinch and pull a small amount of clay out to form a crooked, hooked nose. This takes a little practice and you may need to do it once or twice, to get exactly the look you want. If you don't get it right the first time, don't worry. The good thing about modeling is that you can always roll the clay back up and start again!

7. Now stick the witch's head on top of the purple cape. Push it down well, so the two pieces of clay stick together.

8. Take a ball of black clay and press it in the garlic press, to make lots of little strands of witch's hair. Then attach the hair to the witch's head, arranging it neatly and evenly around the head. Put a few short strands of clay around the front of the head, for a fringe. Save one strand of clay – you will use this later.

TIP!

Darker modeling clay colors such as black and purple sometimes stain lighter colors when stored together. Always store darker and lighter colors separately.

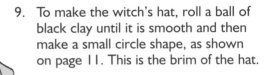

9. To make the witch's hat, roll a ball of black clay until it is smooth and then make a small circle shape, as shown on page 11. This is the brim of the hat.

10. Now use some more black clay to make a cone, as shown on page 8. Stretch the cone out to make a long, pointed hat. Then give it a little bend at the tip, just like a real witch's hat.

11. Attach the cone to the brim of the hat, pressing down gently to make sure that the two pieces stick together. Then place the hat firmly onto the witch's head, so that it sticks to the hair and head.

12. Roll two little pieces of black clay into tiny balls. These are your witch's eyes.

13. Use the remaining strand of black clay to give your witch a mouth. She is now complete – and just waiting for her broom.

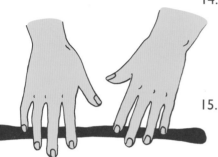

14. Use some more black clay to roll a rope, as shown on Page 10. This will form the witch's broomstick. Don't make the rope too thin, or it will bend and you will not be able to attach the broom straws to it.

15. Now roll a ball of yellow clay and then press it in the garlic press, to form lots of long yellow strands. These will form the straws of the broom.

16. Keep two yellow straws aside. Then bundle the rest of the strands together at one end. Use the knife to trim both ends of the strands, so they are neat and straight.

17. Stick the narrow end of the bunch of yellow strands firmly to the broomstick.

18. Now take the two remaining strands and wrap them once around the place where the broomstick and straws join. Then trim them neatly.

19. The witch's broom is now finished. Place it beside your creepy witch and she's ready to start scaring people!

TIP!

If your witch's broomstick doesn't want to stay straight, try poking a long toothpick up the middle of it. This will help stop the modeling clay from sagging.

MAD MONSTER

Let your imagination go wild and create a mad Halloween monster!

YOU WILL NEED:

- Modeling clay in the color of your choice
- Knife
- Garlic press
- Toothpick

1. Roll all the pieces of clay you will need first, when you create this model. Then put them together to make your monster. First, roll a large piece of clay into a smooth ball and then form a thick sausage shape, as shown on Page 9. Push each end of the sausage against a flat surface, to flatten it. The sausage will form the body of the monster.

2. Roll a smaller amount of clay into a smooth ball. This ball will form the monster's head.

3. Now roll two clay ropes, as shown on Page 10. Make the first rope almost twice as long as the sausage and about half as thick – this rope will form the monster's legs. Make the second rope about one and a half times as long as the thick sausage and a little thinner than the first rope – this rope will form the monster's arms. Cut both ropes in half and push their ends against a flat surface, to flatten them. Then put them aside.

4. Roll four more balls of clay for the monster's feet and hands. Flatten each of the balls slightly, then pinch and mold them into hand and foot shapes.

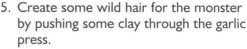

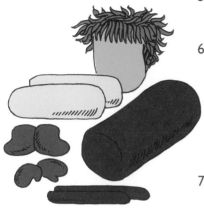

5. Create some wild hair for the monster by pushing some clay through the garlic press.

6. Now you can put all the pieces together. Begin by placing the ball you made for the head on to the sausage body. Press the two pieces of clay gently together, so they stick together. Then use your fingers or the knife to smooth around the join, so it's not so obvious.

7. Next, attach the arms and legs to the monster, again pressing the pieces of modeling clay gently together so they stick well, and smoothing around the joins. Then stick on the hands and feet.

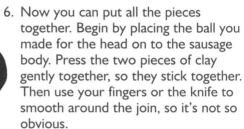

8. Carefully pinch out a nose on the monster's face. Then use the toothpick to give the monster some eyes and a mouth.

9. Finally, stick on the hair. Your monster is complete. What a scary sight!

TIP!

If you have trouble making your monster stand up, you can strengthen its arms and legs by putting toothpicks up inside them, as you did with the witch's broom. Or ask an adult for some small pieces of wire, which also works well.

ANIMAL MAGIC

You can have lots of fun making all sorts of clay animals. There are several different ways to make animals and we'll show you two here.

WOOLLY SHEEP

This farmyard favorite looks really cute.

YOU WILL NEED:

- White modeling clay
- Black modeling clay
- Small fork
- Knife
- Toothpick

1. Take some white clay and roll it into a large ball shape. Continue to roll the ball between the palms of your hands and make a smooth oval shape, as shown on Page 9. This will form the body of your sheep.

2. Now take some more white clay and roll it into a smaller ball. Once you have a smooth ball, carefully pinch and pull the center of one side of the ball to form a rounded, sheep-like nose.

3. To create a lumpy, wooly effect on the sheep, gently use your thumb and forefinger to pinch around the head and body of the sheep. Do not pinch around the sheep's nose – leave it as smooth as possible. Pinch the clay just enough to create an uneven surface on the head and body, rather than creating big lumps of clay on them.

WOOLLY SHEEP

4. Place the head on the front of the body and push the two pieces of clay gently together, so they stick together and the sheep's head stays in place.

5. Using your fingers or the small fork, carefully smooth the join between the sheep's head and neck, so it is not so obvious.

6. Now take some more white clay and roll it out into a rope, as shown on Page 10. Make the rope thick enough to form the legs of the sheep. Cut four small pieces of rope of equal length.

7. Attach each of the legs to the sheep's body, pressing the modeling clay gently together, so the legs and body stick together.

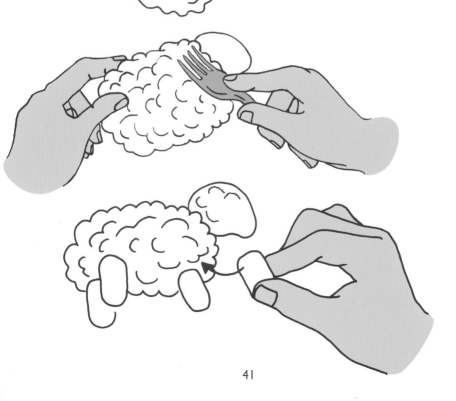

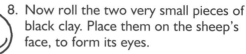

8. Now roll the two very small pieces of black clay. Place them on the sheep's face, to form its eyes.

9. Take two small pieces of white clay and roll them into balls. Then form two small circles, as shown on Page 11. Pinch the ends of the circles to form a flat oval shape, and then attach them to the top of the sheep's head. These are the sheep's ears.

10. Use the small fork to add to the sheep's woolly look by creating small swirls all over its body. Create some extra light swirls on its head, too. You might like to practice creating the swirls first, on a spare piece of modeling clay. Then you will be sure to get them just right when you do them on the sheep.

11. Finally, draw in two nostrils and a mouth on the sheep. Your sheep is now complete!

TIP!

Did you know that sheep are born with cute little tails? You can turn your sheep into a lamb by using any leftover white clay to make it a tail.

PINK PIG

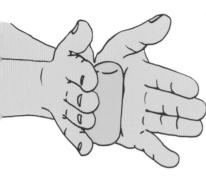

Make this cute pig by using a very old modeling technique to form its legs and neck out of one piece of clay. It's a little harder than the technique you used to make the sheep, but it gives the body and legs a very smooth appearance.

YOU WILL NEED:

- Pink modeling clay
- Knife
- Toothpick

1. Roll and knead some pink clay into a large ball. Work the clay in your hands until it feels smooth. Then form a thick sausage, as shown on Page 9.

2. Now here's the tricky part – but once you've done it a few times, you will find it easy. Using both thumbs, make a small central hollow down the length of the sausage, leaving each end of the sausage a little thicker, as shown. Then pinch out the clay a little way on each side of the hollow. This will be the underside of your pig.

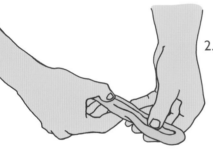

3. Using your thumb and forefinger, carefully pinch out and mold the clay on two sides of the hollow, at one end of the sausage. Stretch the clay out to form two little legs. These are the back legs of the pig.

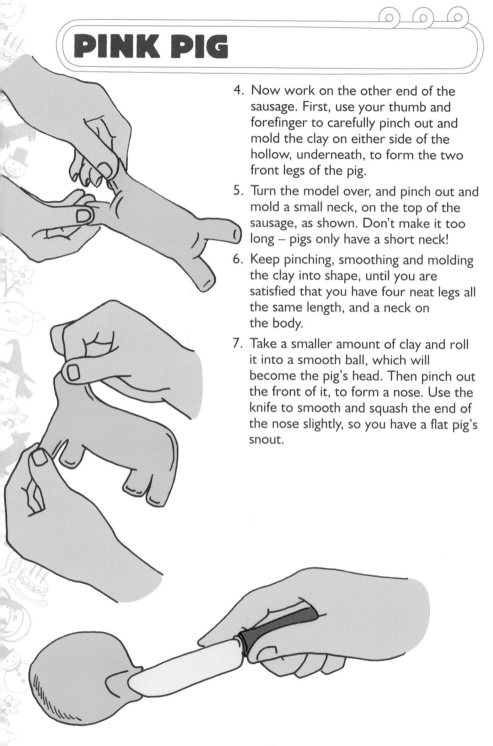

4. Now work on the other end of the sausage. First, use your thumb and forefinger to carefully pinch out and mold the clay on either side of the hollow, underneath, to form the two front legs of the pig.

5. Turn the model over, and pinch out and mold a small neck, on the top of the sausage, as shown. Don't make it too long – pigs only have a short neck!

6. Keep pinching, smoothing and molding the clay into shape, until you are satisfied that you have four neat legs all the same length, and a neck on the body.

7. Take a smaller amount of clay and roll it into a smooth ball, which will become the pig's head. Then pinch out the front of it, to form a nose. Use the knife to smooth and squash the end of the nose slightly, so you have a flat pig's snout.

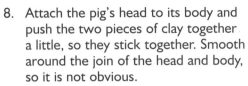

PINK PIG

8. Attach the pig's head to its body and push the two pieces of clay together a little, so they stick together. Smooth around the join of the head and body, so it is not obvious.

9. Roll two very small pieces of clay into balls and form two small circles, as shown on Page 11. Pinch the circles into triangle shapes and place them on the pig's head. These are its ears.

10. Pigs have a cute, corkscrew tail. Make the pig's tail by rolling a very small rope, as shown on Page 10. Then twist the rope into a corkscrew and place it on the pig.

11. Use the toothpick to create two small eyes above the pig's snout. Make two little nostrils and finally, a small mouth underneath the snout. Your cute pig is ready for the farmyard!

TIP!

Most objects you make can be formed with one piece of clay. You can make pots, people and any type of animal in this way – give it a try!

TINY TERRIER

Your friends will all want a little pet like this tiny terrier, when they see yours!

YOU WILL NEED:

- Black modeling clay
- Brown modeling clay, or other lighter color
- Toothpick

1. For this project, use the same technique as you did to make the pig. Just use a little more clay. Roll and knead some black clay into a large ball. Then form a thick sausage, as shown on Page 9.

2. Using both thumbs, make a small central hollow down the length of the sausage, leaving each end of the sausage a little thicker, as shown. Then pinch out the clay a little way on each side of the hollow. This will be the underside of your terrier.

3. Using your thumb and forefinger, carefully pinch out and mold the clay on two sides of the hollow, at the very end of the sausage. Stretch the clay out to form two little legs. This will form the back legs of your terrier.

4. Now pinch and mold a small pointy tail on top of the sausage, above the back legs. Turn the tail up slightly, just like a real terrier's tail.

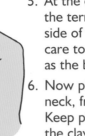

5. At the other end of the sausage, form the terrier's two front legs from either side of the hollow, underneath. Take care to make the legs the same length as the back legs.

6. Now pinch out and mold a small thick neck, from the top of the sausage. Keep pinching, smoothing and molding the clay into shape until you are satisfied that you have four neat legs and a neck on the body.

7. Take some more black clay and roll into a smooth ball, to form the terrier's head. Then pinch out the front of it, to form a rounded doggy nose.

8. Roll two very small pieces of black clay into balls and form two small circles, as shown on Page 11. Pinch the circles into triangle shapes and place them on the terrier's head. Bend the tip of each triangle over slightly. These are its ears.

9. Roll two very small balls of brown clay and attach them to the terrier's head. These are its eyes.

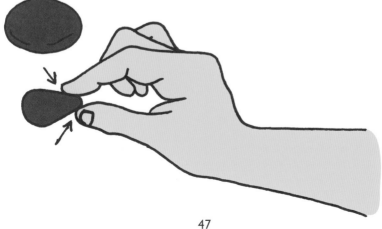

10. Also roll a very small, thin brown rope, as shown on page 10. Cut two tiny pieces from the rope and stick them above the terrier's eyes. These are its eyebrows.

11. Roll a very small ball of black clay and attach it to the tip of the terrier's nose, to complete the head.

12. Now attach the terrier's head to its body and push the two pieces of clay together a little, so they stick together. Use your fingers to smooth around the join of the head and body, so it is not obvious.

13. Use the toothpick to create some small lines on the terrier's body, head and legs, to give it a doggy coat. You now have a new pet!

TIP!

With practice, you will be able to change the shape of the terrier to make any type of dog you want.

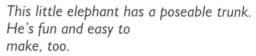
This little elephant has a poseable trunk. He's fun and easy to make, too.

YOU WILL NEED:

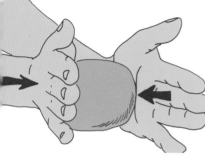

- Gray modeling clay or other color of your choice
- Small piece of wire or pipe cleaner, around 1 1/2 in. (3.8 cm) long (always ask an adult to cut wire or pipe cleaners for you)
- Knife
- Toothpick

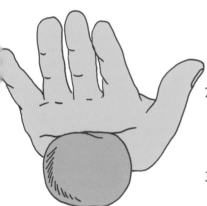

1. Roll all the pieces of clay you will need first when you create this model, as you did for the Mad Monster on Page 38. Then put them together to make your elephant.

2. First, roll a large piece of clay into a smooth ball. Then make an oval shape, as shown on Page 9. Press the two ends of the oval in a little way, so that they look more like an elephant's body.

3. Now roll a smaller ball of clay to create the elephant's head. Flatten the top of the ball slightly. Then put it aside.

4. Roll a clay rope of medium thickness, as shown on Page 10. Then cut four pieces of rope the same length. These are the elephant's legs.

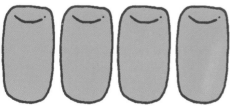

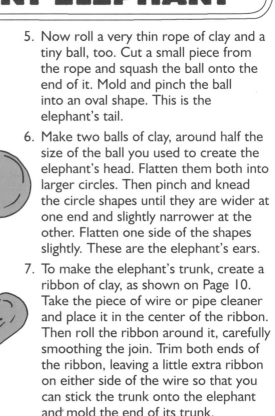

5. Now roll a very thin rope of clay and a tiny ball, too. Cut a small piece from the rope and squash the ball onto the end of it. Mold and pinch the ball into an oval shape. This is the elephant's tail.

6. Make two balls of clay, around half the size of the ball you used to create the elephant's head. Flatten them both into larger circles. Then pinch and knead the circle shapes until they are wider at one end and slightly narrower at the other. Flatten one side of the shapes slightly. These are the elephant's ears.

7. To make the elephant's trunk, create a ribbon of clay, as shown on Page 10. Take the piece of wire or pipe cleaner and place it in the center of the ribbon. Then roll the ribbon around it, carefully smoothing the join. Trim both ends of the ribbon, leaving a little extra ribbon on either side of the wire so that you can stick the trunk onto the elephant and mold the end of its trunk.

8. Now it's time to put the elephant together. First, stick the head to the body, gently pressing the two pieces of clay together so that the head stays in place. Smooth the join between the head and the body with your fingers, so it is not obvious.

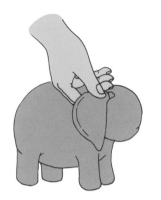

9. Stick the ears carefully to each side of the head, pinching and molding them until they look just right. The ears are one of the hardest parts of this model to get right, so if at first you don't succeed, don't worry. Just squash up that modeling clay and make a new set of ears!

10. Now attach the trunk, smoothing the join between the head and the trunk really well with your fingers, so that it cannot easily be seen. Gently pose the trunk in an upward position, so it looks like the elephant is trumpeting.

11. Attach the elephant's little tail.

12. Finally, use the toothpick to give the elephant some eyes, nostrils at the end of his trunk and a smiley mouth. Add a few lines to the top of his trunk and give him some toenails too, just like a real elephant. Doesn't he look fantastic!

TIP!

Wires and plastic 'skeletons' that are sometimes put in clay models are called armature. You can buy armature from some art, craft and modeling shops.

You can also find stores that sell armature on the Internet. Ask an adult to help you look some up.

ADVANCED PROJECTS

If you've worked your way through the earlier modeling projects in this book, you'll now be ready to try making some more advanced models.

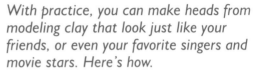

HANDSOME HEADS

With practice, you can make heads from modeling clay that look just like your friends, or even your favorite singers and movie stars. Here's how.

YOU WILL NEED:

- Photo or picture of the person you wish to make a model of
- Large amount of modeling clay, in the color of your choice
- Polystyrene foam craft ball (available from craft stores), or a ball of newspaper covered in plastic wrap, or foil
- Rolling pin, knife and toothpick
- Garlic press

1. Knead a ball of clay between your hands until it is nice and smooth. Then roll it out into a flat slab, around 1/2 in. (1.25 cm) thick.

2. Carefully wrap the slab of clay over the polystyrene craft ball, to form the head. Then gather the ends of the clay together and knead and pinch them into a neck shape.

3. Trim the ends of the neck and then press the neck and head gently down onto a flat surface, so the base of the neck is flat and will sit well on a table.

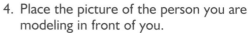

4. Place the picture of the person you are modeling in front of you.

5. Now use the toothpick and mark out rough positions on the head for nose, eyes, mouth and ears. Start with the nose first. This will be your marker for where to put the other parts of the face.

6. Roll a ball of clay and stick it to the place where you have marked out the nose. However, before you do so, take a close look at the picture. Does the person you are making a model of have a big nose, or a small nose? Try to make the nose look just like the one in the picture.

7. Next make the ears and stick them to the model. Then press your thumbs gently into the head to form the eyes. Knead and pinch the clay into shape. Use the toothpick to draw in the irises, pupils, eyelashes and eyebrows.

8. Create the mouth by adding two small ropes of clay and pinching and molding them into the face. Then make some hair with the garlic press. Continue pinching and molding the clay until you are happy with the model. When it is finished, show it to your friends and family!

TIP!

Do not worry if at first, your heads don't look exactly like the people you are modeling. With practice, you will get better and better.

ALIEN PLANET

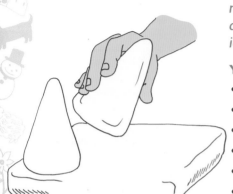

You can create cool alien planets with modeling clay, complete with space ships and monsters. Add your own creative ideas to this basic design.

YOU WILL NEED:

- Wooden board or metal baking tray
- Large amount of white modeling clay
- Black modeling clay
- Red modeling clay
- Green modeling clay
- Bottle caps of different sizes
- Rolling pin, knife and toothpick

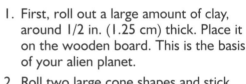

1. First, roll out a large amount of clay, around 1/2 in. (1.25 cm) thick. Place it on the wooden board. This is the basis of your alien planet.

2. Roll two large cone shapes and stick them to the rear of the board, as shown. Smooth the base of each cone, so it blends with the white clay base. Then press a hole in the top of each cone with your thumb. Roll two small balls of red clay and place them in the holes at the top of each cone. You now have two alien volcanoes!

3. Next, take the different sized bottle caps and gently press them into the white clay base, in places. You have now made lots of craters. Make some of the craters deeper than others.

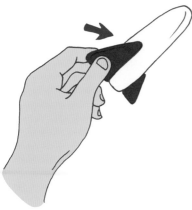

4. Use some more white clay to make a space ship. Roll a thick sausage shape, as shown on Page 9. Then pinch and mold one end of it until it forms a point. Take some black clay and roll it out into a flat slap about 1/4 in. (.75 cm) thick. Cut out some triangle-shaped wings and a tail for the space ship, and stick them on.

5. Now use the green clay to make some aliens. Make several small aliens, using the Ghostly Ghouls model on page 32, the Creepy Witch model on page 34 and the Mad Monster model on Page 38 as a guide. Alternatively, create your own designs from scratch. Make them look as alien as possible by stretching their arms and legs out.

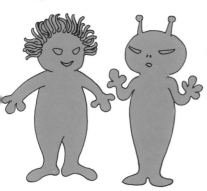

6. Place the models onto the alien planet. You could have them hiding in craters, or behind the volcanoes.

7. Finally, make an astronaut out of some more white clay. Use the Mad Monster model on Page 38 as a guide but make the head a round ball, as the astronaut will be wearing a space suit. Make a small rectangle shape and place it on the astronaut's back. This is the air tank. Then roll out a small flat square shape and stick it to the astronaut's helmet. This is the visor of the helmet. Place the completed astronaut beside the space ship and your planet is complete!

TIP!

Ask an adult to help you find some websites about other planets such as Mars on the Internet. You can look the pictures of the planets on the websites and get ideas for your alien planet models.

APPLE ORCHARD

This flat two-dimensional scene is made in the same way as the Colorful Blooms scene on Page 30.

YOU WILL NEED:

- Small piece of square cardboard (alternatively, a thin square slab of white modeling clay)
- Black modeling clay
- Green modeling clay
- Red modeling clay
- Yellow modeling clay
- White modeling clay
- Rolling pin, garlic press and knife

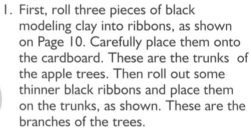

1. First, roll three pieces of black modeling clay into ribbons, as shown on Page 10. Carefully place them onto the cardboard. These are the trunks of the apple trees. Then roll out some thinner black ribbons and place them on the trunks, as shown. These are the branches of the trees.

2. Take some green modeling clay and press it in the garlic press to make lots of strands of green grass. Arrange the grass around the tree trunks, at the bottom of the scene.

3. Use some more green clay and make lots and lots of small circles, as shown on Page 11. Pinch and mold one end of each of the small circles, to form a leaf shape.

4. Arrange all the leaves on the branches of the apple trees.

5. Now make some apples for the trees. Make at least twelve small circles. Make the circles a little larger than the circles you made for the leaves. Then stick them onto the trees – at least four to each tree.

6. Next, let's put a sun in the sky. Using the yellow clay, make a slightly larger circle. This is the center of the sun. Place it in sky, above the apple trees.

7. Make ten very small circles. Then pinch and mold the ends of the circles into triangle shapes. Use the knife to flatten the base of each of the triangle shapes and trim their edges, if you wish. Stick the ten triangle shapes around the sun, as shown.

8. Roll out a thin slab of white modeling clay and carefully use the knife to cut out a fluffy cloud shape. Place the cloud in the sky and your beautiful apple orchard is complete!

TIP!

Make flat two-dimensional scenes with polymer clay. Then you can put them in a frame and hang them on the wall, and they will last for many years.

SALT DOUGH MODELING

Salt dough can be made at home and used to make many different models. Once they have been baked, your models will last for a very long time.

SALT DOUGH RECIPE

Here is a simple salt dough recipe for you to try. Remember – always ask for an adult's help when you want to use the oven!

YOU WILL NEED:

- 4 to 4 1/2 cups flour
- 2 cups salt
- 4 teaspoons non-toxic powder paint in a color of your choice
- 1 1/2 to 2 cups water
- 1 teaspoon vegetable oil
- Large mixing bowl and spoon
- Oven and baking tray
- An adult's help

1. First, mix the flour, salt and powder paint together in the bowl. Make sure the powder paint is spread evenly throughout the mixture.

2. Slowly add the vegetable oil, mixing it through with the spoon.

3. Slowly add one and a half cups of water and stir well, until it becomes a firm dough. If the mixture is too stiff, add some extra water. Add the water a little at a time, so that the mixture does not become too moist. If the mixture is too moist, add some extra flour, a little at a time.

4. Knead the dough until it is completely smooth. Be patient with this part, and make sure all the lumps are out of it. Then you will be able to create better salt dough models.

5. The salt dough is now ready for use. You can use it right away or wrap it in plastic. This recipe will keep in the refrigerator for two to three days.

6. After you have made your models with the dough, place them on a baking tray which has been dusted with flour.

7. Ask an adult to dry your models in an oven at 212° F (100° C). Thinner models will need to be dried for around two hours. Thicker models need to be dried for between two and six hours. Add an extra two hours cooking time for every 1 in. (2.5 cm) dough thickness.

TIP!

Try making salt dough models without any coloring. Then paint them with non-toxic paints after they have been baked.

UNIQUE WALL PLAQUE

This salt dough wall plaque will look fantastic on the door of your room. It's a big project and takes a while to bake, but is well worth the effort!

YOU WILL NEED:

- 2 quantities of plain colored salt dough
- Rolling pin
- Knife and spoon
- Small plate
- Letter stencil (optional)
- Oven and baking tray
- Skewer
- Gold and silver gloss paints (available from craft stores)
- Paint brush
- Old newspaper
- An adult's help

1. Roll out the salt dough into a big ball and then split it in half. Put one half aside and wrap it in plastic – you will use it later.

2. Use the rolling pin to roll out one half of the salt dough into an even slab, until it is about 3/4 in. (2 cm) thick.

3. Place the small plate over the dough and carefully cut around it with the knife, so you have a circular dough shape.

4. Using the handle of the spoon, carefully press a rounded pattern all the way around the edge of the dough. Alternatively, use the top of the spoon or the edge of the knife to create a different pattern of your choice.

5. Use the knife to help you lift the circular piece of salt dough and place it on the baking tray. This will form the back of your plaque.

6. Mix and roll the leftover dough together with the second half of the dough that you put aside earlier, until it is smooth.

7. Roll the dough out flat with the rolling pin, until it is about a 1/2 in. (1.25 cm) thick. Now the fun begins! How will you decorate your plaque? The choice is yours, but we suggest you start with your name, or your initials.

8. Using a letter stencil, carefully mark out your name or initials on the dough with the tip of the skewer. Remove the stencil and then cut the letters out.

9. Stick the letters firmly onto the circular plaque you placed on the baking tray. Make sure they stick very well, or they will fall off after they have been dried in the oven. You can do this by moistening the back of the letters very slightly, before you stick them down.

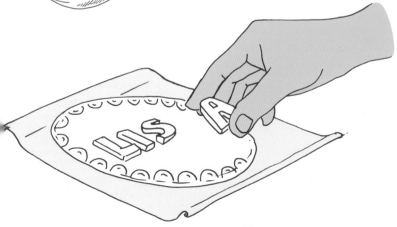

10. Make some cool shapes of your own design – they may be leaves and flowers, robots, monsters, stars and moons, or anything you wish. Then stick them to the plaque, all around the letters.

11. Make a hole in the top of the plaque with the skewer, so you can hang it up. Then ask an adult to place it in an oven at 212°F (100°C) for approximately four hours, or until thoroughly dry. Ask your adult helper to keep checking the model every half hour after the first two hours, to make sure it does not burn.

12. When the plaque is cool and dry, you can paint it. Lay out some old newspaper to protect your work surface. Then place the plaque on the newspaper.

13. Paint the wall plaque in glossy silver and gold colors. If necessary, apply a second coat of paint after the first one has dried, to get a perfect, shiny finish.

TIP!

You could also make an oblong, square or oval plaque if you wish. Oblong shapes are great if you have a longer name and want to put your full name on the plaque, rather than just your initials.

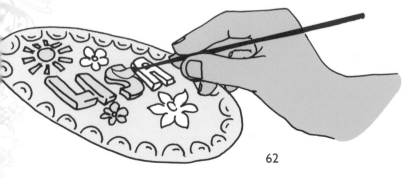